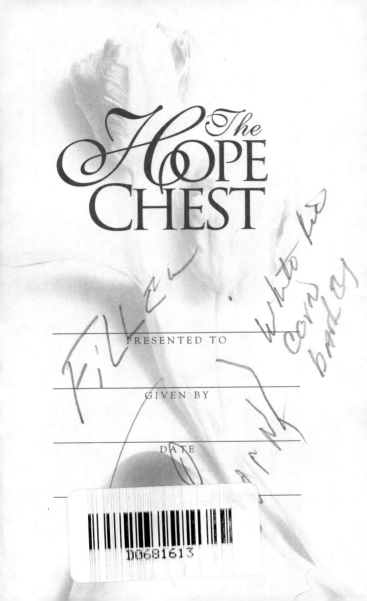

The HOPE CHEST

PRESENTED TO

GIVEN BY

DATE

D0581613

The Hope Chest

A TREASURY OF HOPE
FROM THE
WOMEN OF DESTINY™ BIBLE

Cindy Jacobs
General Editor

Leslyn Musch
Compiler

A Spirit-Filled Life® Product

NELSON

Thomas Nelson Publishers
Nashville

Introduction

The Scriptures are full of hope, and I don't know many women who do not need hope in some area of their lives! Life often contains disappointments, but Romans 5:5 tells us that "hope does not disappoint, because the love of God has been poured out in our hearts by the Holy Spirit who was given to us." Hope keeps us praying, keeps us believing, and keeps us in the love of God and in the comfort of the Holy Spirit.

Perhaps you are familiar with the *Women of Destiny Bible*, which contains its own "Hope Chest"—a list of Scripture references for many of the unique situations women face. Over and over again, women tell me how much those references have helped them in times of need. Just as women often fill a hope chest with natural symbols of hope, these Scriptures represent promises from Jesus Christ, our heavenly Bridegroom, to us, His Bride.

Throughout this small volume, you will find Bible verses that can help you as you

deal with your personal life, your relation-
ship with God, your emotions, your family,
and even your practical needs. All of these
verses are individual treasures from God's
Word, which is "living and powerful . . . and
is a discerner of the thoughts and intents of
the heart" (Hebrews 4:12). At the end of the
book, you will find Scriptures to help you
celebrate your hope and rejoice when God
fulfills His promises to you.

May the Scriptures tucked away in
this hope chest provide you with a constant
source of strength and encouragement.

Cindy Jacobs

General Editor
Women of Destiny Bible

Contents

The Bible: The Book of Your Hope

God: The Source of Your Hope

Hope for Your Relationship with God

Hope for Your Spiritual Growth

Hope for Your Relationships with Others

Hope When You Feel

Hope When You Need

Hope When You Are

Hope to Overcome

Celebrating Your Hope

The Bible:
The Book
of
Your Hope

Your Enduring Hope

The grass withers, the flower fades,
But the word of our God stands forever.

ISAIAH 40:8

Heaven and earth will pass away, but My
words will by no means pass away.

MARK 13:31

So now, brethren, I commend you to God
and to the word of His grace, which is able
to build you up and give you an inheritance
among all those who are sanctified.

ACTS 20:32

All Scripture is given by inspiration of God,
and is profitable for doctrine, for reproof, for
correction, for instruction in righteousness,
that the man of God may be complete, thoroughly equipped for every good work.

2 TIMOTHY 3:16, 17

For the word of God is living and powerful,
and sharper than any two-edged sword,
piercing even to the division of soul and
spirit, and of joints and marrow, and is a
discerner of the thoughts and intents of
the heart.

HEBREWS 4:12

Your Hope for Comfort

God is our refuge and strength,
A very present help in trouble. PSALM 46:1

Remember the word to Your servant,
Upon which You have caused me
   to hope.
This is my comfort in my affliction,
For Your word has given me life.

PSALM 119:49, 50

For whatever things were written before
were written for our learning, that we
through the patience and comfort of the
Scriptures might have hope. ROMANS 15:4

But as it is written:

"Eye has not seen, nor ear heard,
Nor have entered into the heart
   of man
The things which God has prepared
   for those who love Him."

I CORINTHIANS 2:9

Now to Him who is able to keep you from
    stumbling,
And to present you faultless
Before the presence of His glory with
    exceeding joy,
To God our Savior,
Who alone is wise,
Be glory and majesty,
Dominion and power,
Both now and forever.
Amen.   JUDE 24, 25

Your Hope for Guidance

This Book of the Law shall not depart from
your mouth, but you shall meditate in it day
and night, that you may observe to do
according to all that is written in it. For then
you will make your way prosperous, and
then you will have good success.   JOSHUA 1:8

The law of the LORD is perfect, converting
    the soul;
The testimony of the LORD is sure, making
    wise the simple;
The statutes of the LORD are right, rejoicing
    the heart;
The commandment of the LORD is pure,
    enlightening the eyes.   PSALM 19:7, 8

Your word is a lamp to my feet
And a light to my path.   PSALM 119:105

When you roam, they will lead you;
When you sleep, they will keep you;
And when you awake, they will speak
    with you.
For the commandment is a lamp,
And the law a light;
Reproofs of instruction are the way of life.

PROVERBS 6:22, 23

Then Jesus said to those Jews who believed Him, "If you abide in My word, you are My disciples indeed. And you shall know the truth, and the truth shall make you free."

JOHN 8:31, 32

The Strength of Your Hope

As for God, His way is perfect;
The word of the LORD is proven;
He is a shield to all who trust in Him.

PSALM 18:30

The counsel of the LORD stands
    forever,
The plans of His heart to all
    generations.

PSALM 33:11

Heaven and earth will pass away, but My words will by no means pass away.

MARK 13:31

So now, brethren, I commend you to God and to the word of His grace, which is able to build you up and give you an inheritance among all those who are sanctified.

ACTS 20:32

In Him you also trusted, after you heard the word of truth, the gospel of your salvation; in whom also, having believed, you were sealed with the Holy Spirit of promise, who is the guarantee of our inheritance until the redemption of the purchased possession, to the praise of His glory.

EPHESIANS 1:13, 14

God:
The Source
of
Your Hope

Is Faithful

Then Moses called Joshua and said to him in the sight of all Israel, "Be strong and of good courage, for you must go with this people to the land which the LORD has sworn to their fathers to give them, and you shall cause them to inherit it. And the LORD, He is the One who goes before you. He will be with you, He will not leave you nor forsake you; do not fear nor be dismayed."

DEUTERONOMY 31:7, 8

Your mercy, O LORD, is in the heavens;
Your faithfulness reaches to the clouds.

PSALM 36:5

I will sing of the mercies of the LORD forever;
With my mouth will I make known Your
        faithfulness to all generations.
For I have said, "Mercy shall be built up
        forever;
Your faithfulness You shall establish in the
        very heavens." PSALM 89:1, 2

God is faithful, by whom you were called into the fellowship of His Son, Jesus Christ our Lord. 1 CORINTHIANS 1:9

And Moses indeed was faithful in all His house as a servant, for a testimony of those things which would be spoken afterward, but Christ as a Son over His own house, whose house we are if we hold fast the confidence and the rejoicing of the hope firm to the end. HEBREWS 3:5, 6

Is Gracious

For the LORD God is a sun and shield;
The LORD will give grace and glory;
No good thing will He withhold
From those who walk uprightly. PSALM 84:11

But the free gift is not like the offense. For if by the one man's offense many died, much more the grace of God and the gift by the grace of the one Man, Jesus Christ, abounded to many. ROMANS 5:15

For sin shall not have dominion over you, for you are not under law but under grace.
ROMANS 6:14

God . . . has saved us and called us with a holy calling, not according to our works, but according to His own purpose and grace which was given to us in Christ Jesus before time began. 2 TIMOTHY 1:8, 9

For we do not have a High Priest who cannot sympathize with our weaknesses, but was in all points tempted as we are, yet without sin. Let us therefore come boldly to the throne of grace, that we may obtain mercy and find grace to help in time of need.   HEBREWS 4:15, 16

Is Merciful

Oh, give thanks to the LORD, for He is good!
For His mercy endures forever.
                    1 CHRONICLES 16:34

The LORD is merciful and gracious,
Slow to anger, and abounding in mercy.
                    PSALM 103:8

You are my God, and I will praise You;
You are my God, I will exalt You.

Oh, give thanks to the LORD, for He is good!
For His mercy endures forever.
                    PSALM 118:28, 29

Let the wicked forsake his way,
And the unrighteous man his thoughts;
Let him return to the LORD,
And He will have mercy on him;
And to our God,
For He will abundantly pardon.   ISAIAH 55:7

Blessed be the God and Father of our Lord Jesus Christ, who according to His abundant mercy has begotten us again to a living hope through the resurrection of Jesus Christ from the dead, to an inheritance incorruptible and undefiled and that does not fade away, reserved in heaven for you, who are kept by the power of God through faith for salvation ready to be revealed in the last time.

1 PETER 1:3–5

Is Righteous

He is the Rock, His work is perfect;
For all His ways are justice,
A God of truth and without injustice;
Righteous and upright is He.

DEUTERONOMY 32:4

You have performed Your words,
For You are righteous.

NEHEMIAH 9:8b

For the LORD is righteous,
He loves righteousness;
His countenance beholds the upright.

PSALM 11:7

Righteous are You, O LORD, when I plead
with You.

JEREMIAH 12:1a

And I heard another from the altar saying, "Even so, Lord God Almighty, true and righteous are Your judgments."

REVELATION 16:7

Loves You

Since you were precious in My sight,
You have been honored,
And I have loved you;
Therefore I will give men for you,
And people for your life.

ISAIAH 43:4

The LORD has appeared of old to me,
     saying:
"Yes, I have loved you with an everlasting
     love;
Therefore with lovingkindness I have
     drawn you."

JEREMIAH 31:3

For God so loved the world that He gave His only begotten Son, that whoever believes in Him should not perish but have everlasting life. For God did not send His Son into the world to condemn the world, but that the world through Him might be saved.

JOHN 3:16, 17

Now hope does not disappoint, because the love of God has been poured out in our hearts by the Holy Spirit who was given to us. For when we were still without strength, in due time Christ died for the ungodly. For scarcely for a righteous man will one die; yet perhaps for a good man someone would even dare to die. But God demonstrates His own love toward us, in that while we were still sinners, Christ died for us.   ROMANS 5:5–8

But when the kindness and the love of God our Savior toward man appeared, not by works of righteousness which we have done, but according to His mercy He saved us, through the washing of regeneration and renewing of the Holy Spirit, whom He poured out on us abundantly through Jesus Christ our Savior, that having been justified by His grace we should become heirs according to the hope of eternal life.

TITUS 3:4–7

Forgives You

"Come now, and let us reason together,"
  Says the LORD,
"Though your sins are like scarlet,
  They shall be as white as snow;
  Though they are red like crimson,
  They shall be as wool."   ISAIAH 1:18

16

I, even I, am He who blots out your
transgressions for My own sake;
And I will not remember your sins.

ISAIAH 43:25

I will cleanse them from all their iniquity by
which they have sinned against Me, and I
will pardon all their iniquities by which they
have sinned and by which they have trans-
gressed against Me.   JEREMIAH 33:8

Much more then, having now been justified
by His blood, we shall be saved from wrath
through Him. For if when we were enemies
we were reconciled to God through the
death of His Son, much more, having been
reconciled, we shall be saved by His life.

ROMANS 5:9, 10

And you, who once were alienated and enemies in your mind by wicked works, yet now
He has reconciled in the body of His flesh
through death, to present you holy, and
blameless, and above reproach in His
sight—if indeed you continue in the faith,
grounded and steadfast, and are not moved
away from the hope of the gospel which you
heard, which was preached to every creature under heaven, of which I, Paul, became
a minister.   COLOSSIANS 1:21–23

Accepts You

All that the Father gives Me will come to Me, and the one who comes to Me I will by no means cast out. JOHN 6:37

For the Scripture says, "Whoever believes on Him will not be put to shame."
ROMANS 10:11

Now all things are of God, who has reconciled us to Himself through Jesus Christ, and has given us the ministry of reconciliation, that is, that God was in Christ reconciling the world to Himself, not imputing their trespasses to them, and has committed to us the word of reconciliation.
2 CORINTHIANS 5:18, 19

But now in Christ Jesus you who once were far off have been brought near by the blood of Christ. For He Himself is our peace.
EPHESIANS 2:13, 14a

Coming to Him as to a living stone, rejected indeed by men, but chosen by God and precious, you also, as living stones, are being built up a spiritual house, a holy priesthood, to offer up spiritual sacrifices acceptable to God through Jesus Christ.
1 PETER 2:4, 5

Guides You

For this commandment which I command
you today is not too mysterious for you, nor
is it far off . . . But the word is very near you,
in your mouth and in your heart, that you
may do it.   DEUTERONOMY 30:11, 14

The steps of a good man are ordered by
    the LORD,
And He delights in his way.   PSALM 37:23

For this is God,
Our God forever and ever;
He will be our guide
Even to death.   PSALM 48:14

In all your ways acknowledge Him,
And He shall direct your paths.   PROVERBS 3:6

A man's heart plans his way,
But the LORD directs his steps.   PROVERBS 16:9

Keeps You

The LORD bless you and keep you;
The LORD make His face shine upon you,
And be gracious to you;
The LORD lift up His countenance upon you,
And give you peace.   NUMBERS 6:24–26

You will keep him in perfect peace,
Whose mind is stayed on You,
Because he trusts in You.
Trust in the LORD forever,
For in YAH, the LORD, is everlasting
strength. ISAIAH 26:3, 4

For I am persuaded that neither death nor
life, nor angels nor principalities nor powers, nor things present nor things to come,
nor height nor depth, nor any other created
thing, shall be able to separate us from the
love of God which is in Christ Jesus our
Lord. ROMANS 8:38, 39

Blessed be the God and Father of our Lord
Jesus Christ, who according to His abundant
mercy has begotten us again to a living
hope through the resurrection of Jesus
Christ from the dead, to an inheritance
incorruptible and undefiled and that does
not fade away, reserved in heaven for you,
who are kept by the power of God through
faith for salvation ready to be revealed in
the last time. 1 PETER 1:3–5

Now to Him who is able to keep you from
    stumbling,
And to present you faultless
Before the presence of His glory with
    exceeding joy,
To God our Savior,
Who alone is wise,
Be glory and majesty,
Dominion and power,
Both now and forever.
Amen.   JUDE 24, 25

Hears Your Prayers

Delight yourself also in the LORD,
And He shall give you the desires of
    your heart.   PSALM 37:4

As for me, I will call upon God,
And the LORD shall save me.
Evening and morning and at noon
I will pray, and cry aloud,
And He shall hear my voice.   PSALM 55:16, 17

Thus says the LORD who made it, the LORD
who formed it to establish it (the LORD is
His name): "Call to Me, and I will answer
you, and show you great and mighty things,
which you do not know."   JEREMIAH 33:2, 3

Ask, and it will be given to you; seek, and you will find; knock, and it will be opened to you. For everyone who asks receives, and he who seeks finds, and to him who knocks it will be opened.   MATTHEW 7:7, 8

If you abide in Me, and My words abide in you, you will ask what you desire, and it shall be done for you.   JOHN 15:7

Will Keep His Word

Blessed be the LORD, who has given rest to His people Israel, according to all that He promised. There has not failed one word of all His good promise, which He promised through His servant Moses.   I KINGS 8:56

For He remembered His holy promise, And Abraham His servant.   PSALM 105:42

The grass withers, the flower fades, But the word of our God stands forever.

ISAIAH 40:8

Calling a bird of prey from the east, The man who executes My counsel, from a
    far country.
Indeed I have spoken it;
I will also bring it to pass.
I have purposed it;
I will also do it.   ISAIAH 46:11

Jesus Christ is the same yesterday, today, and forever. HEBREWS 13:8

Will Be with You

And He said, "My Presence will go with you, and I will give you rest." EXODUS 33:14

And the LORD, He is the One who goes before you. He will be with you, He will not leave you nor forsake you; do not fear nor be dismayed. DEUTERONOMY 31:8

Yea, though I walk through the valley of the
shadow of death,
I will fear no evil;
For You are with me;
Your rod and Your staff, they
comfort me. PSALM 23:4

The sun shall no longer be your light
by day,
Nor for brightness shall the moon
give light to you;
But the LORD will be to you an
everlasting light,
And your God your glory. ISAIAH 60:19

Jesus answered and said to him, "If anyone loves Me, he will keep My word; and My Father will love him, and We will come to him and make Our home with him."

JOHN 14:23

Hope

for

Your

Relationship with God

Repenting of Sin

Then Peter said to them, "Repent, and let every one of you be baptized in the name of Jesus Christ for the remission of sins; and you shall receive the gift of the Holy Spirit. For the promise is to you and to your children, and to all who are afar off, as many as the Lord our God will call." ACTS 2:38, 39

Repent therefore and be converted, that your sins may be blotted out, so that times of refreshing may come from the presence of the Lord. ACTS 3:19

Or do you despise the riches of His goodness, forbearance, and longsuffering, not knowing that the goodness of God leads you to repentance? ROMANS 2:4

The Lord is not slack concerning His promise, as some count slackness, but is longsuffering toward us, not willing that any should perish but that all should come to repentance. 2 PETER 3:9

If we say that we have no sin, we deceive ourselves, and the truth is not in us. If we confess our sins, He is faithful and just to forgive us our sins and to cleanse us from all unrighteousness. 1 JOHN 1:8, 9

Exercising Faith

So then faith comes by hearing, and hearing by the word of God.   ROMANS 10:17

Now faith is the substance of things hoped for, the evidence of things not seen.

HEBREWS 11:1

Therefore . . . let us run with endurance the race that is set before us, looking unto Jesus, the author and finisher of our faith, who for the joy that was set before Him endured the cross, despising the shame, and has sat down at the right hand of the throne of God.   HEBREWS 12:1, 2

In this you greatly rejoice, though now for a little while, if need be, you have been grieved by various trials, that the genuineness of your faith, being much more precious than gold that perishes, though it is tested by fire, may be found to praise, honor, and glory at the revelation of Jesus Christ, whom having not seen you love. Though now you do not see Him, yet believing, you rejoice with joy inexpressible and full of glory, receiving the end of your faith—the salvation of your souls.

1 PETER 1:6–9

For whatever is born of God overcomes the world. And this is the victory that has overcome the world—our faith. 1 JOHN 5:4

Receiving Salvation

For God so loved the world that He gave His only begotten Son, that whoever believes in Him should not perish but have everlasting life. For God did not send His Son into the world to condemn the world, but that the world through Him might be saved. JOHN 3:16, 17

Therefore by the deeds of the law no flesh will be justified in His sight, for by the law is the knowledge of sin. But now the righteousness of God apart from the law is revealed, being witnessed by the Law and the Prophets, even the righteousness of God, through faith in Jesus Christ, to all and on all who believe. For there is no difference; for all have sinned and fall short of the glory of God, being justified freely by His grace through the redemption that is in Christ Jesus. ROMANS 3:20–24

For when we were still without strength, in due time Christ died for the ungodly. For scarcely for a righteous man will one die; yet perhaps for a good man someone would even dare to die. But God demonstrates His own love toward us, in that while we were still sinners, Christ died for us.   ROMANS 5:6–8

In Him we have redemption through His blood, the forgiveness of sins, according to the riches of His grace.   EPHESIANS 1:7

The Lord is not slack concerning His promise, as some count slackness, but is longsuffering toward us, not willing that any should perish but that all should come to repentance.   2 PETER 3:9

Being Part of the Family of God

For the LORD will not forsake His people, for His great name's sake, because it has pleased the LORD to make you His people.

1 SAMUEL 12:22

I will be a Father to you,
And you shall be My sons and daughters,
Says the LORD Almighty.   2 CORINTHIANS 6:18

For you are all sons of God through faith in Christ Jesus.   GALATIANS 3:26

Blessed be the God and Father of our Lord Jesus Christ, who has blessed us with every spiritual blessing in the heavenly places in Christ, . . . having predestined us to adoption as sons by Jesus Christ to Himself, according to the good pleasure of His will, to the praise of the glory of His grace, by which He made us accepted in the Beloved.
                                    EPHESIANS 1:3, 5, 6

Behold what manner of love the Father has bestowed on us, that we should be called children of God!   1 JOHN 3:1

Being Filled with the Holy Spirit

I indeed baptize you with water unto repentance, but He who is coming after me is mightier than I, whose sandals I am not worthy to carry. He will baptize you with the Holy Spirit and fire.   MATTHEW 3:11

And I will pray the Father, and He will give you another Helper, that He may abide with you forever—the Spirit of truth, whom the world cannot receive, because it neither sees Him nor knows Him; but you know Him, for He dwells with you and will be in you. JOHN 14:16, 17

So Jesus said to them again, "Peace to you! As the Father has sent Me, I also send you." And when He had said this, He breathed on them, and said to them, "Receive the Holy Spirit." JOHN 20:21, 22

But you shall receive power when the Holy Spirit has come upon you; and you shall be witnesses to Me in Jerusalem, and in all Judea and Samaria, and to the end of the earth. ACTS 1:8

When the Day of Pentecost had fully come, they were all with one accord in one place. And suddenly there came a sound from heaven, as of a rushing mighty wind, and it filled the whole house where they were sitting. Then there appeared to them divided tongues, as of fire, and one sat upon each of them. And they were all filled with the Holy Spirit and began to speak with other tongues, as the Spirit gave them utterance. ACTS 2:1–4

Reading and Studying Scripture

This Book of the Law shall not depart from your mouth, but you shall meditate in it day and night, that you may observe to do according to all that is written in it. For then you will make your way prosperous, and then you will have good success.   JOSHUA 1:8

With my whole heart I have sought You;
Oh, let me not wander from Your
    commandments!
Your word I have hidden in my heart,
That I might not sin against You!
Blessed are You, O LORD!
Teach me Your statutes!   PSALM 119:10–12

Be diligent to present yourself approved to God, a worker who does not need to be ashamed, rightly dividing the word of truth.
2 TIMOTHY 2:15

All Scripture is given by inspiration of God, and is profitable for doctrine, for reproof, for correction, for instruction in righteousness.
2 TIMOTHY 3:16

But be doers of the word, and not hearers only, deceiving yourselves. For if anyone is a hearer of the word and not a doer, he is like a man observing his natural face in a mirror; for he observes himself, goes away, and immediately forgets what kind of man he was. But he who looks into the perfect law of liberty and continues in it, and is not a forgetful hearer but a doer of the work, this one will be blessed in what he does.

JAMES 1:22–25

Practicing Prayer

Call to Me, and I will answer you, and show you great and mighty things, which you do not know.

JEREMIAH 33:3

Again I say to you that if two of you agree on earth concerning anything that they ask, it will be done for them by My Father in heaven. For where two or three are gathered together in My name, I am there in the midst of them.

MATTHEW 18:19, 20

Therefore I say to you, whatever things you ask when you pray, believe that you receive them, and you will have them.

MARK 11:24

Likewise the Spirit also helps in our weaknesses. For we do not know what we should pray for as we ought, but the Spirit Himself makes intercession for us with groanings which cannot be uttered.   ROMANS 8:26

Seeing then that we have a great High Priest who has passed through the heavens, Jesus the Son of God, let us hold fast our confession. For we do not have a High Priest who cannot sympathize with our weaknesses, but was in all points tempted as we are, yet without sin. Let us therefore come boldly to the throne of grace, that we may obtain mercy and find grace to help in time of need.   HEBREWS 4:14–16

Hope

for

Your

Spiritual Growth

Experiencing Deliverance

I sought the LORD, and He heard me,
And delivered me from all my fears.
They looked to Him and were radiant,
And their faces were not ashamed.

PSALM 34:4, 5

Many are the afflictions of the righteous,
But the LORD delivers him out of them all.

PSALM 34:19

No temptation has overtaken you except
such as is common to man; but God is faithful, who will not allow you to be tempted
beyond what you are able, but with the
temptation will also make the way of
escape, that you may be able to bear it.

1 CORINTHIANS 10:13

Grace to you and peace from God the
Father and our Lord Jesus Christ, who gave
Himself for our sins, that He might deliver
us from this present evil age, according to
the will of our God and Father.

GALATIANS 1:3, 4

And the Lord will deliver me from every evil
work and preserve me for His heavenly
kingdom. To Him be glory forever and ever.
Amen!

2 TIMOTHY 4:18

Forgiving Others

Then Peter came to Him and said, "Lord, how often shall my brother sin against me, and I forgive him? Up to seven times?" Jesus said to him, "I do not say to you, up to seven times, but up to seventy times seven."
MATTHEW 18:21, 22

And whenever you stand praying, if you have anything against anyone, forgive him, that your Father in heaven may also forgive you your trespasses.
MARK 11:25

Therefore be merciful, just as your Father also is merciful. Judge not, and you shall not be judged. Condemn not, and you shall not be condemned. Forgive, and you will be forgiven.
LUKE 6:36, 37

Let all bitterness, wrath, anger, clamor, and evil speaking be put away from you, with all malice. And be kind to one another, tenderhearted, forgiving one another, even as God in Christ forgave you.
EPHESIANS 4:31, 32

Therefore, as the elect of God, holy and beloved, put on tender mercies, kindness, humility, meekness, longsuffering; bearing with one another, and forgiving one another, if anyone has a complaint against another; even as Christ forgave you, so you also must do. But above all these things put on love, which is the bond of perfection.

COLOSSIANS 3:12–14

Living in Freedom

And you shall know the truth, and the truth shall make you free.   JOHN 8:32

Therefore if the Son makes you free, you shall be free indeed.   JOHN 8:36

There is therefore now no condemnation to those who are in Christ Jesus, who do not walk according to the flesh, but according to the Spirit. For the law of the Spirit of life in Christ Jesus has made me free from the law of sin and death.   ROMANS 8:1, 2

Now the Lord is the Spirit; and where the Spirit of the Lord is, there is liberty.

2 CORINTHIANS 3:17

Stand fast therefore in the liberty by which Christ has made us free, and do not be entangled again with a yoke of bondage.

GALATIANS 5:1

Gaining Spiritual Maturity

But we all, with unveiled face, beholding as in a mirror the glory of the Lord, are being transformed into the same image from glory to glory, just as by the Spirit of the Lord.

2 CORINTHIANS 3:18

For this reason I bow my knees to the Father of our Lord Jesus Christ . . . that He would grant you, according to the riches of His glory, to be strengthened with might through His Spirit in the inner man, that Christ may dwell in your hearts through faith; that you, being rooted and grounded in love, may be able to comprehend with all the saints what is the width and length and depth and height—to know the love of Christ which passes knowledge; that you may be filled with all the fullness of God.

EPHESIANS 3:14, 16–19

He who has begun a good work in you will complete it until the day of Jesus Christ.

PHILIPPIANS 1:6b

Therefore, laying aside all malice, all deceit, hypocrisy, envy, and all evil speaking, as newborn babes, desire the pure milk of the word, that you may grow thereby, if indeed you have tasted that the Lord is gracious.

1 PETER 2:1–3

But also for this very reason, giving all diligence, add to your faith virtue, to virtue knowledge, to knowledge self-control, to self-control perseverance, to perseverance godliness, to godliness brotherly kindness, and to brotherly kindness love. For if these things are yours and abound, you will be neither barren nor unfruitful in the knowledge of our Lord Jesus Christ.

2 PETER 1:5–8

Hearing God's Voice

And you said: "Surely the LORD our God has shown us His glory and His greatness, and we have heard His voice from the midst of the fire. We have seen this day that God speaks with man; yet he still lives."

DEUTERONOMY 5:24

Then He said, "Go out, and stand on the mountain before the LORD." And behold, the LORD passed by, and a great and strong wind tore into the mountains and broke the rocks in pieces before the LORD, but the LORD was not in the wind; and after the wind an earthquake, but the LORD was not in the earthquake; and after the earthquake a fire, but the LORD was not in the fire; and after the fire a still small voice.   1 KINGS 19:11, 12

And when he brings out his own sheep, he goes before them; and the sheep follow him, for they know his voice. Yet they will by no means follow a stranger, but will flee from him, for they do not know the voice of strangers.   JOHN 10:4, 5

And other sheep I have which are not of this fold; them also I must bring, and they will hear My voice; and there will be one flock and one shepherd.   JOHN 10:16

My sheep hear My voice, and I know them, and they follow Me.   JOHN 10:27

Knowing God's Will

If you seek her as silver,
And search for her as for hidden treasures;
Then you will understand the fear of
    the LORD,
And find the knowledge of God.
For the LORD gives wisdom;
From His mouth come knowledge and
    understanding.   PROVERBS 2:4–6

Trust in the LORD with all your heart,
And lean not on your own understanding;
In all your ways acknowledge Him,
And He shall direct your paths.
    PROVERBS 3:5, 6

Evil men do not understand justice,
But those who seek the LORD
    understand all.   PROVERBS 28:5

I will bring the blind by a way they did
    not know;
I will lead them in paths they have not
    known.
I will make darkness light before them,
And crooked places straight.
These things I will do for them,
And not forsake them.   ISAIAH 42:16

However, when He, the Spirit of truth, has come, He will guide you into all truth; for He will not speak on His own authority, but whatever He hears He will speak; and He will tell you things to come. JOHN 16:13

Surrendering to God

If My people who are called by My name will humble themselves, and pray and seek My face, and turn from their wicked ways, then I will hear from heaven, and will forgive their sin and heal their land.

2 CHRONICLES 7:14

For thus says the High and
    Lofty One
Who inhabits eternity, whose
    name is Holy:
"I dwell in the high and holy place,
With him who has a contrite and
    humble spirit,
To revive the spirit of the humble,
And to revive the heart of the
    contrite ones."

ISAIAH 57:15

Take My yoke upon you and learn from Me, for I am gentle and lowly in heart, and you will find rest for your souls. MATTHEW 11:29

Therefore whoever humbles himself as this little child is the greatest in the kingdom of heaven.   MATTHEW 18:4

Humble yourselves in the sight of the Lord, and He will lift you up.   JAMES 4:10

Obeying God

So Samuel said:

"Has the LORD as great delight in burnt
      offerings and sacrifices,
As in obeying the voice of the LORD?
Behold, to obey is better than sacrifice,
And to heed than the fat of rams."

                    1 SAMUEL 15:22

Like an earring of gold and an ornament of
      fine gold
Is a wise rebuker to an obedient ear.

                    PROVERBS 25:12

He has shown you, O man, what is good;
And what does the LORD require of you
But to do justly,
To love mercy,
And to walk humbly with your God?

                    MICAH 6:8

If you love Me, keep My commandments.

                    JOHN 14:15

Therefore, my beloved, as you have always obeyed, not as in my presence only, but now much more in my absence, work out your own salvation with fear and trembling; for it is God who works in you both to will and to do for His good pleasure.

PHILIPPIANS 2:12, 13

Discerning Truth

Who is the man that fears the LORD?
Him shall He teach in the way He chooses.

PSALM 25:12

I will instruct you and teach you in the way
you should go;
I will guide you with My eye.   PSALM 32:8

The entirety of Your word is truth,
And every one of Your righteous judgments
endures forever.   PSALM 119:160

Then Jesus said to those Jews who believed Him, "If you abide in My word, you are My disciples indeed. And you shall know the truth, and the truth shall make you free."

JOHN 8:31, 32

Jesus said to him, "I am the way, the truth, and the life. No one comes to the Father except through Me."   JOHN 14:6

Walking in Holiness

Then I will give them one heart, and I will
put a new spirit within them, and take the
stony heart out of their flesh, and give them
a heart of flesh, that they may walk in My
statutes and keep My judgments and do
them; and they shall be My people, and I
will be their God.   EZEKIEL 11:19, 20

Blessed is the Lord God of Israel
For He has visited and redeemed
      His people, . . .
To grant us that we,
Being delivered from the hand of
      our enemies,
Might serve Him without fear,
In holiness and righteousness
      before Him all the days
      of our life.   LUKE 1:68, 74, 75

Therefore, having these promises, beloved,
let us cleanse ourselves from all filthiness of
the flesh and spirit, perfecting holiness in
the fear of God.   2 CORINTHIANS 7:1

Finally, brethren, whatever things are true, whatever things are noble, whatever things are just, whatever things are pure, whatever things are lovely, whatever things are of good report, if there is any virtue and if there is anything praiseworthy—meditate on these things. The things which you learned and received and heard and saw in me, these do, and the God of peace will be with you.   PHILIPPIANS 4:8, 9

Therefore if anyone cleanses himself from the latter, he will be a vessel for honor, sanctified and useful for the Master, prepared for every good work.   2 TIMOTHY 2:21

Increasing in Faith

So then faith comes by hearing, and hearing by the word of God.   ROMANS 10:17

And my speech and my preaching were not with persuasive words of human wisdom, but in demonstration of the Spirit and of power, that your faith should not be in the wisdom of men but in the power of God.
                    1 CORINTHIANS 2:4, 5

For by grace you have been saved through faith, and that not of yourselves; it is the gift of God. EPHESIANS 2:8

Now faith is the substance of things hoped for, the evidence of things not seen. HEBREWS 11:1

In this you greatly rejoice, though now for a little while, if need be, you have been grieved by various trials, that the genuineness of your faith, being much more precious than gold that perishes, though it is tested by fire, may be found to praise, honor, and glory at the revelation of Jesus Christ. 1 PETER 1:6, 7

Hope

for

Your

Relationships

with Others

Being a Witness

The fruit of the righteous is a tree of life,
And he who wins souls is wise.

PROVERBS 11:30

And Jesus came and spoke to them, saying,
"All authority has been given to Me in heaven
and on earth. Go therefore and make
disciples of all the nations, baptizing them
in the name of the Father and of the Son
and of the Holy Spirit, teaching them to
observe all things that I have commanded
you; and lo, I am with you always, even to
the end of the age." Amen.   MATTHEW 28:18–20

But you shall receive power when the Holy
Spirit has come upon you; and you shall be
witnesses to Me in Jerusalem, and in all
Judea and Samaria, and to the end of the
earth.   ACTS 1:8

I charge you therefore before God and the
Lord Jesus Christ, who will judge the living
and the dead at His appearing and His kingdom: Preach the word! Be ready in season
and out of season. Convince, rebuke, exhort,
with all longsuffering and teaching . . . But
you be watchful in all things, endure afflictions, do the work of an evangelist, fulfill
your ministry.   2 TIMOTHY 4:1, 2, 5

But sanctify the Lord God in your hearts, and always be ready to give a defense to everyone who asks you a reason for the hope that is in you, with meekness and fear; having a good conscience, that when they defame you as evildoers, those who revile your good conduct in Christ may be ashamed.   1 PETER 3:15, 16

Praying for Unsaved Loved Ones

Train up a child in the way he should go, And when he is old he will not depart from it.   PROVERBS 22:6

For the Son of Man has come to save that which was lost. What do you think? If a man has a hundred sheep, and one of them goes astray, does he not leave the ninety-nine and go to the mountains to seek the one that is straying? And if he should find it, assuredly, I say to you, he rejoices more over that sheep than over the ninety-nine that did not go astray. Even so it is not the will of your Father who is in heaven that one of these little ones should perish.

MATTHEW 18:11–14

And a woman who has a husband who does not believe, if he is willing to live with her, let her not divorce him. For the unbelieving husband is sanctified by the wife, and the unbelieving wife is sanctified by the husband; otherwise your children would be unclean, but now they are holy.

1 CORINTHIANS 7:13, 14

Wives, likewise, be submissive to your own husbands, that even if some do not obey the word, they, without a word, may be won by the conduct of their wives, when they observe your chaste conduct accompanied by fear.

1 PETER 3:1, 2

The Lord is not slack concerning His promise, as some count slackness, but is longsuffering toward us, not willing that any should perish but that all should come to repentance.

2 PETER 3:9

Sharing with Neighbors

LORD, who may abide in Your
  tabernacle?
Who may dwell in Your holy hill?

He who walks uprightly,
  And works righteousness,
  And speaks the truth in his heart;
He who does not backbite with
    his tongue,
  Nor does evil to his neighbor,
  Nor does he take up a reproach
    against his friend.   PSALM 15:1–3

Like a madman who throws firebrands,
    arrows, and death,
Is the man who deceives his
    neighbor,
And says, "I was only joking!"
                          PROVERBS 26:18, 19

Jesus said to him, "'You shall love the LORD
your God with all your heart, with all your
soul, and with all your mind.' This is the first
and great commandment. And the second is
like it: 'You shall love your neighbor as
yourself.'"   MATTHEW 22:37–39

Owe no one anything except to love one another, for he who loves another has fulfilled the law. For the commandments, "You shall not commit adultery," "You shall not murder," "You shall not steal," "You shall not bear false witness," "You shall not covet," and if there is any other commandment, are all summed up in this saying, namely, "You shall love your neighbor as yourself." ROMANS 13:8, 9

Therefore, putting away lying, "Let each one of you speak truth with his neighbor," for we are members of one another. EPHESIANS 4:25

Caring for the Elderly

Children's children are the crown of old
    men,
And the glory of children is their father.
PROVERBS 17:6

The glory of young men is their strength,
And the splendor of old men is their
    gray head. PROVERBS 20:29

Do not rebuke an older man, but exhort him as a father, younger men as brothers, older women as mothers, younger women as sisters, with all purity. 1 TIMOTHY 5:1, 2

Let the elders who rule well be counted
worthy of double honor, especially those
who labor in the word and doctrine.

I TIMOTHY 5:17

Likewise you younger people, submit yourselves to your elders. Yes, all of you be
submissive to one another, and be clothed
with humility.

I PETER 5:5a

Being a Daughter

Honor your father and your mother, as the
LORD your God has commanded you, that
your days may be long, and that it may be
well with you in the land which the LORD
your God is giving you.

DEUTERONOMY 5:16

My son, hear the instruction of your father,
And do not forsake the law of your mother;
For they will be a graceful ornament on
    your head,
And chains about your neck.

PROVERBS 1:8, 9

My son, keep your father's command,
And do not forsake the law of your mother.
Bind them continually upon your heart;
Tie them around your neck.
When you roam, they will lead you;
When you sleep, they will keep you;
And when you awake, they will speak
    with you.

PROVERBS 6:20–22

Listen to your father who begot you,
And do not despise your mother when she
is old. . . .

The father of the righteous will greatly
rejoice,
And he who begets a wise child will delight
in him.
Let your father and your mother be glad,
And let her who bore you rejoice.

PROVERBS 23:22, 24, 25

Children, obey your parents in all things, for
this is well pleasing to the Lord.

COLOSSIANS 3:20

Being a Wife

Your wife shall be like a fruitful vine
In the very heart of your house,
Your children like olive plants
All around your table.   PSALM 128:3

An excellent wife is the crown of her
husband,
But she who causes shame is like rottenness
in his bones.   PROVERBS 12:4

The wise woman builds her house,
But the foolish pulls it down with her hands.

PROVERBS 14:1

Who can find a virtuous wife?
For her worth is far above rubies.
The heart of her husband safely
     trusts her;
So he will have no lack of gain.
She does him good and not evil
All the days of her life. . . .
Charm is deceitful and beauty
     is passing,
But a woman who fears the LORD,
     she shall be praised.

PROVERBS 31:10–12, 30

Let the husband render to his wife the
affection due her, and likewise also the wife
to her husband.   1 CORINTHIANS 7:3

Dealing with Marital Problems

Choose for yourselves this day whom you
will serve, whether the gods which your
fathers served that were on the other side
of the River, or the gods of the Amorites, in
whose land you dwell. But as for me and my
house, we will serve the LORD.   JOSHUA 24:15b

I acknowledged my sin to You,
And my iniquity I have not hidden.
I said, "I will confess my transgressions to
    the LORD,"
And You forgave the iniquity of my sin.

Selah

For this cause everyone who is godly shall
    pray to You
In a time when You may be found;
Surely in a flood of great waters
They shall not come near him.
You are my hiding place;
You shall preserve me from trouble;
You shall surround me with songs of
    deliverance.

Selah

PSALM 32:5–7

Love suffers long and is kind; love does not
envy; love does not parade itself, is not
puffed up; does not behave rudely, does
not seek its own, is not provoked, thinks no
evil; does not rejoice in iniquity, but rejoices in the truth; bears all things, believes all
things, hopes all things, endures all things.
Love never fails.

1 CORINTHIANS 13:4–8a

Let all bitterness, wrath, anger, clamor, and
evil speaking be put away from you, with all
malice. And be kind to one another, tenderhearted, forgiving one another, even as God
in Christ forgave you.

EPHESIANS 4:31, 32

But He gives more grace. Therefore He says:

"God resists the proud,
 But gives grace to the humble."

Therefore submit to God. Resist the devil
and he will flee from you. Draw near to God
and He will draw near to you.   JAMES 4:6–8a

Working Through a Spouse's Unfaithfulness

You are my hiding place;
You shall preserve me from trouble;
You shall surround me with songs of
     deliverance.   Selah
                              PSALM 32:7

The LORD is near to those who have a
     broken heart,
And saves such as have a contrite spirit.
                              PSALM 34:18

He heals the brokenhearted
And binds up their wounds.   PSALM 147:3

Do not say, "I will do to him just as he has
     done to me;
I will render to the man according to
     his work."   PROVERBS 24:29

Repay no one evil for evil. Have regard for good things in the sight of all men. If it is possible, as much as depends on you, live peaceably with all men. Beloved, do not avenge yourselves, but rather give place to wrath; for it is written, "Vengeance is Mine, I will repay," says the Lord.   ROMANS 12:17–19

Coping with an Alcoholic Spouse

May the LORD answer you in the day
    of trouble;
May the name of the God of Jacob
    defend you;
May He send you help from the
    sanctuary,
And strengthen you out of Zion.   PSALM 20:1, 2

For in the time of trouble
He shall hide me in His pavilion;
In the secret place of His tabernacle
He shall hide me;
He shall set me high upon a rock.   PSALM 27:5

God is our refuge and strength,
A very present help in trouble.   PSALM 46:1

In that day it shall be said to
    Jerusalem:
"Do not fear;
Zion, let not your hands
    be weak.
The LORD your God in your midst,
The Mighty One, will save;
He will rejoice over you
    with gladness,
He will quiet you with His love,
He will rejoice over you
    with singing."   ZEPHANIAH 3:16, 17

Peace I leave with you, My peace I give to
you; not as the world gives do I give to you.
Let not your heart be troubled, neither let it
be afraid.   JOHN 14:27

Dealing with Divorce

The secret of the LORD is with those who
    fear Him,
And He will show them His covenant.
My eyes are ever toward the LORD,
For He shall pluck my feet out of the net.

Turn Yourself to me, and have mercy on me,
For I am desolate and afflicted.
The troubles of my heart have enlarged;
Bring me out of my distresses!
Look on my affliction and my pain,
And forgive all my sins.   PSALM 25:14–18

Trust in the LORD with all
   your heart,
And lean not on your own
   understanding;
In all your ways acknowledge Him,
And He shall direct your paths.

PROVERBS 3:5, 6

But from the beginning of the creation, God
"made them male and female." "For this
reason a man shall leave his father and
mother and be joined to his wife, and the
two shall become one flesh"; so then they
are no longer two, but one flesh. Therefore
what God has joined together, let not man
separate.   MARK 10:6–9

Be anxious for nothing, but in everything by
prayer and supplication, with thanksgiving,
let your requests be made known to God;
and the peace of God, which surpasses all
understanding, will guard your hearts and
minds through Christ Jesus.

PHILIPPIANS 4:6, 7

Therefore humble yourselves under the mighty hand of God, that He may exalt you in due time, casting all your care upon Him, for He cares for you. Be sober, be vigilant; because your adversary the devil walks about like a roaring lion, seeking whom he may devour. Resist him, steadfast in the faith, knowing that the same sufferings are experienced by your brotherhood in the world.   1 PETER 5:6–9

Being a Mother

And these words which I command you today shall be in your heart. You shall teach them diligently to your children, and shall talk of them when you sit in your house, when you walk by the way, when you lie down, and when you rise up. You shall bind them as a sign on your hand, and they shall be as frontlets between your eyes. You shall write them on the doorposts of your house and on your gates.   DEUTERONOMY 6:6–9

Blessed is every one who fears the LORD,
Who walks in His ways.

When you eat the labor of your hands,
You shall be happy, and it shall be well
          with you.
Your wife shall be like a fruitful vine
In the very heart of your house,
Your children like olive plants
All around your table.   PSALM 128:1–3

Train up a child in the way he should go,
And when he is old he will not depart
    from it.   PROVERBS 22:6

The rod and rebuke give wisdom,
But a child left to himself brings shame to
    his mother. . . .

Correct your son, and he will give you rest;
Yes, he will give delight to your soul.
                        PROVERBS 29:15, 17

Now for the third time I am ready to come
to you. And I will not be burdensome to
you; for I do not seek yours, but you. For
the children ought not to lay up for the parents, but the parents for the children.
                        2 CORINTHIANS 12:14

Handling Rebellious Children

He who covers his sins will not prosper,
But whoever confesses and forsakes them
    will have mercy.   PROVERBS 28:13

I will heal their backsliding,
I will love them freely,
For My anger has turned away from him.
                                HOSEA 14:4

No temptation has overtaken you except such as is common to man; but God is faithful, who will not allow you to be tempted beyond what you are able, but with the temptation will also make the way of escape, that you may be able to bear it.

1 CORINTHIANS 10:13

For we do not have a High Priest who cannot sympathize with our weaknesses, but was in all points tempted as we are, yet without sin. Let us therefore come boldly to the throne of grace, that we may obtain mercy and find grace to help in time of need.

HEBREWS 4:15, 16

Therefore do not cast away your confidence, which has great reward. For you have need of endurance, so that after you have done the will of God, you may receive the promise.

HEBREWS 10:35, 36

Dealing with Family Problems

Therefore you shall lay up these words of mine in your heart and in your soul, and bind them as a sign on your hand, and they shall be as frontlets between your eyes. You shall teach them to your children, speaking of them when you sit in your house, when you walk by the way, when you lie down, and when you rise up. And you shall write them on the doorposts of your house and on your gates, that your days and the days of your children may be multiplied in the land of which the LORD swore to your fathers to give them, like the days of the heavens above the earth.   DEUTERONOMY 11:18–21

God is our refuge and strength,
A very present help in trouble.   PSALM 46:1

The rod and rebuke give wisdom,
But a child left to himself brings shame to
     his mother. . . .

Correct your son, and he will give you rest;
Yes, he will give delight to your soul.
                              PROVERBS 29:15, 17

The LORD is good,
A stronghold in the day of trouble;
And He knows those who trust in Him.

NAHUM 1:7

Therefore humble yourselves under the mighty hand of God, that He may exalt you in due time, casting all your care upon Him, for He cares for you.   1 PETER 5:6, 7

Facing a Potential Abortion

So God created man in His own image; in the image of God He created him; male and female He created them.   GENESIS 1:27

I call heaven and earth as witnesses today against you, that I have set before you life and death, blessing and cursing; therefore choose life, that both you and your descendants may live.   DEUTERONOMY 30:19

For You formed my inward parts;
You covered me in my mother's womb.
I will praise You, for I am fearfully and
    wonderfully made;
Marvelous are Your works,
And that my soul knows very well.
My frame was not hidden from You,
When I was made in secret,
And skillfully wrought in the lowest parts of
    the earth.
Your eyes saw my substance, being yet
    unformed.
And in Your book they all were written,
The days fashioned for me,
When as yet there were none of them.

PSALM 139:13–16

Listen, O coastlands, to Me,
And take heed, you peoples from afar!
The LORD has called Me from the womb;
From the matrix of My mother He has made
    mention of My name.   ISAIAH 49:1

Before I formed you in the womb I
    knew you;
Before you were born I sanctified you;
I ordained you a prophet to the nations.

JEREMIAH 1:5

Hope

When

You

Feel . . .

Afraid

He who dwells in the secret place of the
    Most High
Shall abide under the shadow of the
    Almighty. . . .
You shall not be afraid of the terror
    by night,
Nor of the arrow that flies by day,
Nor of the pestilence that walks in darkness,
Nor of the destruction that lays waste
    at noonday.

A thousand may fall at your side,
And ten thousand at your right hand;
But it shall not come near you.

PSALM 91:1, 5–7

Say to those who are fearful-hearted,
"Be strong, do not fear!
Behold, your God will come with vengeance,
With the recompense of God;
He will come and save you."   ISAIAH 35:4

Peace I leave with you, My peace I give to
you; not as the world gives do I give to you.
Let not your heart be troubled, neither let it
be afraid.   JOHN 14:27

For you did not receive the spirit of
bondage again to fear, but you received the
Spirit of adoption by whom we cry out,
"Abba, Father."   ROMANS 8:15

For God has not given us a spirit of fear, but of power and of love and of a sound mind.

2 TIMOTHY 1:7

Lonely

The LORD also will be a refuge for the
    oppressed,
A refuge in times of trouble.
And those who know Your name will put
    their trust in You;
For You, LORD, have not forsaken those who
    seek You.

PSALM 9:9, 10

Cast your burden on the LORD,
And He shall sustain you;
He shall never permit the righteous to
    be moved.

PSALM 55:22

Fear not, for I am with you;
Be not dismayed, for I am your God.
I will strengthen you,
Yes, I will help you,
I will uphold you with My righteous
    right hand.

ISAIAH 41:10

And I will pray the Father, and He will give you another Helper, that He may abide with you forever—the Spirit of truth, whom the world cannot receive, because it neither sees Him nor knows Him; but you know Him, for He dwells with you and will be in you. I will not leave you orphans; I will come to you. JOHN 14:16–18

For I am persuaded that neither death nor life, nor angels nor principalities nor powers, nor things present nor things to come, nor height nor depth, nor any other created thing, shall be able to separate us from the love of God which is in Christ Jesus our Lord. ROMANS 8:38, 39

Anxious and Worried

In the multitude of my anxieties
    within me,
Your comforts delight my soul. PSALM 94:19

Therefore do not worry, saying, "What shall we eat?" or "What shall we drink?" or "What shall we wear?" For after all these things the Gentiles seek. For your heavenly Father knows that you need all these things. But seek first the kingdom of God and His righteousness, and all these things shall be added to you. Therefore do not worry about tomorrow, for tomorrow will worry about its own things. Sufficient for the day is its own trouble.   MATTHEW 6:31–34

But when they deliver you up, do not worry about how or what you should speak. For it will be given to you in that hour what you should speak; for it is not you who speak, but the Spirit of your Father who speaks in you.   MATTHEW 10:19, 20

Consider the ravens, for they neither sow nor reap, which have neither storehouse nor barn; and God feeds them. Of how much more value are you than the birds? And which of you by worrying can add one cubit to his stature? If you then are not able to do the least, why are you anxious for the rest? Consider the lilies, how they grow: they neither toil nor spin; and yet I say to you, even Solomon in all his glory was not arrayed like one of these. If then God so clothes the grass, which today is in the field and tomorrow is thrown into the oven, how much more will He clothe you, O you of little faith?

LUKE 12:24–28

Be anxious for nothing, but in everything by prayer and supplication, with thanksgiving, let your requests be made known to God; and the peace of God, which surpasses all understanding, will guard your hearts and minds through Christ Jesus.   PHILIPPIANS 4:6, 7

Unhappy

Why are you cast down, O my soul?
And why are you disquieted within me?
Hope in God;
For I shall yet praise Him,
The help of my countenance and my God.

PSALM 43:5

Those who sow in tears
Shall reap in joy.

PSALM 126:5

He heals the brokenhearted
And binds up their wounds.

PSALM 147:3

For the people shall dwell in Zion at
Jerusalem;
You shall weep no more.
He will be very gracious to you at the sound
of your cry;
When He hears it, He will answer you.

ISAIAH 30:19

Therefore you now have sorrow; but I will
see you again and your heart will rejoice,
and your joy no one will take from you.

JOHN 16:22

Grief

Precious in the sight of the LORD
Is the death of His saints.

PSALM 116:15

So the ransomed of the LORD shall return,
And come to Zion with singing,
With everlasting joy on their heads.
They shall obtain joy and gladness;
Sorrow and sighing shall flee away.

ISAIAH 51:11

"O Death, where is your sting?
O Hades, where is your victory?"

The sting of death is sin, and the strength of sin is the law. But thanks be to God, who gives us the victory through our Lord Jesus Christ.   1 CORINTHIANS 15:55–57

But I do not want you to be ignorant, brethren, concerning those who have fallen asleep, lest you sorrow as others who have no hope. For if we believe that Jesus died and rose again, even so God will bring with Him those who sleep in Jesus.

1 THESSALONIANS 4:13, 14

And God will wipe away every tear from their eyes; there shall be no more death, nor sorrow, nor crying. There shall be no more pain, for the former things have passed away.   REVELATION 21:4

Depressed

Fear not, for I am with you;
Be not dismayed, for I am your God.
I will strengthen you,
Yes, I will help you,
I will uphold you with My righteous
     right hand.   ISAIAH 41:10

Yet I will not forget you.
See, I have inscribed you on the palms of
   My hands;
Your walls are continually before Me.

ISAIAH 49:15b, 16

The LORD . . . has sent Me . . .
To console those who mourn in Zion,
To give them beauty for ashes,
The oil of joy for mourning,
The garment of praise for the spirit
   of heaviness;
That they may be called trees
   of righteousness,
The planting of the LORD, that He may
   be glorified. ISAIAH 61:1, 3

Likewise the Spirit also helps in our weaknesses. For we do not know what we should
pray for as we ought, but the Spirit Himself
makes intercession for us with groanings
which cannot be uttered. Now He who
searches the hearts knows what the mind of
the Spirit is, because He makes intercession
for the saints according to the will of God.

ROMANS 8:26, 27

Finally, brethren, whatever things are true, whatever things are noble, whatever things are just, whatever things are pure, whatever things are lovely, whatever things are of good report, if there is any virtue and if there is anything praiseworthy—meditate on these things.   PHILIPPIANS 4:8

Angry

Rest in the LORD, and wait patiently for Him;
Do not fret because of him who prospers in
     his way,
Because of the man who brings wicked
     schemes to pass.
Cease from anger, and forsake wrath;
Do not fret—it only causes harm.
                              PSALM 37:7, 8

He who is slow to wrath has great
     understanding,
But he who is impulsive exalts folly.
                              PROVERBS 14:29

An angry man stirs up strife,
And a furious man abounds in transgression.
                              PROVERBS 29:22

For we do not have a High Priest who cannot sympathize with our weaknesses, but was in all points tempted as we are, yet without sin. Let us therefore come boldly to the throne of grace, that we may obtain mercy and find grace to help in time of need. HEBREWS 4:15, 16

So then, my beloved brethren, let every man be swift to hear, slow to speak, slow to wrath; for the wrath of man does not produce the righteousness of God. JAMES 1:19, 20

Bitter

I make this covenant and this oath, not with you alone, but with him who stands here with us today before the LORD our God, as well as with him who is not here with us today . . . so that there may not be among you man or woman or family or tribe, whose heart turns away today from the LORD our God, to go and serve the gods of these nations, and that there may not be among you a root bearing bitterness or wormwood.

DEUTERONOMY 29:14, 18

For the LORD saw that the affliction of Israel was very bitter; and whether bond or free, there was no helper for Israel. And the LORD did not say that He would blot out the name of Israel from under heaven; but He saved them by the hand of Jeroboam the son of Joash.   2 KINGS 14:26, 27

Indeed it was for my own peace
That I had great bitterness;
But You have lovingly delivered my soul
        from the pit of corruption,
For You have cast all my sins behind
        Your back.   ISAIAH 38:17

Let all bitterness, wrath, anger, clamor, and evil speaking be put away from you, with all malice.   EPHESIANS 4:31

Pursue peace with all people, and holiness, without which no one will see the Lord: looking carefully lest anyone fall short of the grace of God; lest any root of bitterness springing up cause trouble, and by this many become defiled.   HEBREWS 12:14, 15

Frustrated

Commit your way to the LORD,
Trust also in Him,
And He shall bring it to pass.
He shall bring forth your righteousness as
    the light,
And your justice as the noonday.

Rest in the LORD, and wait patiently
    for Him;
Do not fret because of him who prospers in
    his way,
Because of the man who brings wicked
    schemes to pass.
Cease from anger, and forsake wrath;
Do not fret—it only causes harm.

PSALM 37:5–8

You will keep him in perfect peace,
Whose mind is stayed on You,
Because he trusts in You.   ISAIAH 26:3

Now may the Lord direct your hearts into
the love of God and into the patience
of Christ.   2 THESSALONIANS 3:5

For where envy and self-seeking exist, confusion and every evil thing are there. But the wisdom that is from above is first pure, then peaceable, gentle, willing to yield, full of mercy and good fruits, without partiality and without hypocrisy. Now the fruit of righteousness is sown in peace by those who make peace.   JAMES 3:16–18

Beloved, do not think it strange concerning the fiery trial which is to try you, as though some strange thing happened to you; but rejoice to the extent that you partake of Christ's sufferings, that when His glory is revealed, you may also be glad with exceeding joy.   1 PETER 4:12, 13

Insecure

My people will dwell in a peaceful
    habitation,
In secure dwellings, and in quiet
    resting places.   ISAIAH 32:18

My Father, who has given them to Me, is greater than all; and no one is able to snatch them out of My Father's hand.

JOHN 10:29

Yet in all these things we are more than conquerors through Him who loved us.

ROMANS 8:37

I thank my God upon every remembrance of you, . . . being confident of this very thing, that He who has begun a good work in you will complete it until the day of Jesus Christ.

PHILIPPIANS 1:3, 6

You are of God, little children, and have overcome them, because He who is in you is greater than he who is in the world.

1 JOHN 4:4

Guilty

Blessed is he whose transgression
    is forgiven,
Whose sin is covered.
Blessed is the man to whom the LORD does
    not impute iniquity,
And in whose spirit there is no deceit.

PSALM 32:1, 2

But God demonstrates His own love toward us, in that while we were still sinners, Christ died for us. . . . And not only that, but we also rejoice in God through our Lord Jesus Christ, through whom we have now received the reconciliation.

ROMANS 5:8, 11

Therefore, as through one man's offense judgment came to all men, resulting in condemnation, even so through one Man's righteous act the free gift came to all men, resulting in justification of life. For as by one man's disobedience many were made sinners, so also by one Man's obedience many will be made righteous.

ROMANS 5:18, 19

Who shall bring a charge against God's elect? It is God who justifies. Who is he who condemns? It is Christ who died, and furthermore is also risen, who is even at the right hand of God, who also makes intercession for us.

ROMANS 8:33, 34

For godly sorrow produces repentance leading to salvation, not to be regretted; but the sorrow of the world produces death.

2 CORINTHIANS 7:10

Condemnation

There is therefore now no condemnation to those who are in Christ Jesus, who do not walk according to the flesh, but according to the Spirit. For the law of the Spirit of life in Christ Jesus has made me free from the law of sin and death.

ROMANS 8:1, 2

For I am persuaded that neither death nor life, nor angels nor principalities nor powers, nor things present nor things to come, nor height nor depth, nor any other created thing, shall be able to separate us from the love of God which is in Christ Jesus our Lord.   ROMANS 8:38, 39

And such were some of you. But you were washed, but you were sanctified, but you were justified in the name of the Lord Jesus and by the Spirit of our God.

I CORINTHIANS 6:11

If we confess our sins, He is faithful and just to forgive us our sins and to cleanse us from all unrighteousness.   I JOHN 1:9

My little children, these things I write to you, so that you may not sin. And if anyone sins, we have an Advocate with the Father, Jesus Christ the righteous. And He Himself is the propitiation for our sins, and not for ours only but also for the whole world.

I JOHN 2:1, 2

Worthless

O LORD, You have searched me and
    known me.
You know my sitting down and my rising up;
You understand my thought afar off.
You comprehend my path and my
    lying down,
And are acquainted with all my ways.
For there is not a word on my tongue,
But behold, O LORD, You know it altogether.

PSALM 139:1–4

For I know the thoughts that I think toward
you, says the LORD, thoughts of peace and
not of evil, to give you a future and a hope.

JEREMIAH 29:11

Are not two sparrows sold for a copper coin?
And not one of them falls to the ground
apart from your Father's will. But the very
hairs of your head are all numbered. Do not
fear therefore; you are of more value than
many sparrows.

MATTHEW 10:29–31

For you were bought at a price; therefore
glorify God in your body and in your spirit,
which are God's.

1 CORINTHIANS 6:20

By this we know love, because He laid down
His life for us. And we also ought to lay
down our lives for the brethren.

1 JOHN 3:16

Hope
When
You
Need . . .

A Miracle

Again I say to you that if two of you agree
on earth concerning anything that they
ask, it will be done for them by My Father
in heaven.   MATTHEW 18:19

Jesus said to him, "If you can believe, all
things are possible to him who believes."
Immediately the father of the child cried out
and said with tears, "Lord, I believe; help
my unbelief!"   MARK 9:23, 24

Most assuredly, I say to you, he who
believes in Me, the works that I do he will
do also; and greater works than these he
will do, because I go to My Father. And
whatever you ask in My name, that I will do,
that the Father may be glorified in the Son.
If you ask anything in My name, I will do it.
                                   JOHN 14:12–14

Now to Him who is able to do exceedingly
abundantly above all that we ask or think,
according to the power that works in us, to
Him be glory in the church by Christ Jesus
to all generations, forever and ever. Amen.
                                   EPHESIANS 3:20, 21

Is anyone among you sick? Let him call for the elders of the church, and let them pray over him, anointing him with oil in the name of the Lord. . . . Confess your trespasses to one another, and pray for one another, that you may be healed. The effective, fervent prayer of a righteous man avails much.

JAMES 5:14, 16

Provision

I have been young, and now am old;
Yet I have not seen the righteous forsaken,
Nor his descendants begging bread.
He is ever merciful, and lends;
And his descendants are blessed.

PSALM 37:25, 26

The LORD will not allow the righteous soul
to famish,
But He casts away the desire of the wicked.

PROVERBS 10:3

But seek first the kingdom of God and His righteousness, and all these things shall be added to you.

MATTHEW 6:33

And God is able to make all grace abound toward you, that you, always having all sufficiency in all things, may have an abundance for every good work.

2 CORINTHIANS 9:8

And my God shall supply all your need according to His riches in glory by Christ Jesus.   PHILIPPIANS 4:19

Patience

And not only that, but we also glory in tribulations, knowing that tribulation produces perseverance; and perseverance, character; and character, hope. Now hope does not disappoint, because the love of God has been poured out in our hearts by the Holy Spirit who was given to us.   ROMANS 5:3–5

For whatever things were written before were written for our learning, that we through the patience and comfort of the Scriptures might have hope. Now may the God of patience and comfort grant you to be like-minded toward one another, according to Christ Jesus.   ROMANS 15:4, 5

And we desire that each one of you show the same diligence to the full assurance of hope until the end, that you do not become sluggish, but imitate those who through faith and patience inherit the promises.
          HEBREWS 6:11, 12

Therefore do not cast away your confidence, which has great reward. For you have need of endurance, so that after you have done the will of God, you may receive the promise:

"For yet a little while,
And He who is coming will come and will
        not tarry."   HEBREWS 10:35–37

My brethren, count it all joy when you fall into various trials, knowing that the testing of your faith produces patience. But let patience have its perfect work, that you may be perfect and complete, lacking nothing.
                                        JAMES 1:2–4

Strength

The LORD will give strength to His people;
The LORD will bless His people
        with peace.   PSALM 29:11

Be of good courage,
And He shall strengthen your heart,
All you who hope in the LORD.   PSALM 31:24

In the day when I cried out, You
        answered me,
And made me bold with strength
        in my soul.   PSALM 138:3

He gives power to the weak,
And to those who have no might He
increases strength. ISAIAH 40:29

But those who wait on the LORD
Shall renew their strength;
They shall mount up with wings like eagles,
They shall run and not be weary,
They shall walk and not faint. ISAIAH 40:31

Encouragement

I would have lost heart, unless I had
believed
That I would see the goodness of
the LORD
In the land of the living.

Wait on the LORD;
Be of good courage,
And He shall strengthen your heart;
Wait, I say, on the LORD! PSALM 27:13, 14

Though I walk in the midst of trouble, You
will revive me;
You will stretch out Your hand
Against the wrath of my enemies,
And Your right hand will save me.

PSALM 138:7

And let us not grow weary while doing good,
for in due season we shall reap if we do not
lose heart. GALATIANS 6:9

He who has begun a good work in you will complete it until the day of Jesus Christ.

PHILIPPIANS 1:6b

Therefore do not cast away your confidence, which has great reward. For you have need of endurance, so that after you have done the will of God, you may receive the promise.

HEBREWS 10:35, 36

To Know You Are Loved

But now, thus says the LORD, who created
    you, O Jacob,
And He who formed you, O Israel:
"Fear not, for I have redeemed you;
I have called you by your name;
You are Mine."

ISAIAH 43:1

For I know the thoughts that I think toward you, says the LORD, thoughts of peace and not of evil, to give you a future and a hope.

JEREMIAH 29:11

The LORD your God in your midst,
The Mighty One, will save;
He will rejoice over you with gladness,
He will quiet you with His love,
He will rejoice over you with singing.

ZEPHANIAH 3:17

For I am persuaded that neither death nor life, nor angels nor principalities nor powers, nor things present nor things to come, nor height nor depth, nor any other created thing, shall be able to separate us from the love of God which is in Christ Jesus our Lord. ROMANS 8:38, 39

And we have known and believed the love that God has for us. God is love, and he who abides in love abides in God, and God in him. 1 JOHN 4:16

Hope

Behold, the eye of the LORD is on
    those who fear Him,
On those who hope in His mercy,
To deliver their soul from death,
And to keep them alive in famine.

Our soul waits for the LORD;
He is our help and our shield.
For our heart shall rejoice in Him,
Because we have trusted in His
    holy name.
Let Your mercy, O LORD, be upon us,
Just as we hope in You. PSALM 33:18–22

Why are you cast down, O my soul?
And why are you disquieted within me?
Hope in God;
For I shall yet praise Him,
The help of my countenance and my God.

PSALM 42:11

In You, O LORD, I put my trust;
Let me never be put to shame.
Deliver me in Your righteousness, and
    cause me to escape;
Incline Your ear to me, and save me.

PSALM 71:1, 2

Now hope does not disappoint, because
the love of God has been poured out in
our hearts by the Holy Spirit who was given
to us.   ROMANS 5:5

Thus God . . . confirmed it by an oath, that
by two immutable things, in which it is
impossible for God to lie, we might have
strong consolation, who have fled for refuge
to lay hold of the hope set before us. This
hope we have as an anchor of the soul, both
sure and steadfast, and which enters the
Presence behind the veil.   HEBREWS 6:17–19

Perseverance

He gives power to the weak,
And to those who have no might He
    increases strength.
Even the youths shall faint and
    be weary,
And the young men shall utterly fall,
But those who wait on the LORD
Shall renew their strength;
They shall mount up with wings
    like eagles,
They shall run and not be weary,
They shall walk and not faint.   ISAIAH 40:29–31

For we have become partakers of Christ if
we hold the beginning of our confidence
steadfast to the end.   HEBREWS 3:14

Therefore do not cast away your confidence,
which has great reward. For you have need
of endurance, so that after you have done
the will of God, you may receive the
promise.   HEBREWS 10:35, 36

Now for a little while, if need be, you have been grieved by various trials, that the genuineness of your faith, being much more precious than gold that perishes, though it is tested by fire, may be found to praise, honor, and glory at the revelation of Jesus Christ, whom having not seen you love. Though now you do not see Him, yet believing, you rejoice with joy inexpressible and full of glory, receiving the end of your faith—the salvation of your souls.

1 PETER 1:6b–9

He who overcomes shall be clothed in white garments, and I will not blot out his name from the Book of Life; but I will confess his name before My Father and before His angels.

REVELATION 3:5

Protection

And he said:

"The LORD is my rock and my fortress and my
    deliverer;
The God of my strength, in whom I will trust;
My shield and the horn of my salvation,
My stronghold and my refuge;
My Savior, You save me from violence.

2 SAMUEL 22:2, 3

He who dwells in the secret place of the
    Most High
Shall abide under the shadow of the
    Almighty.
I will say of the LORD, "He is my refuge and
    my fortress;
My God, in Him I will trust." . . .

He shall cover you with His feathers,
And under His wings you shall take refuge;
His truth shall be your shield and buckler.

PSALM 91:1, 2, 4

In the fear of the LORD there is strong
    confidence,
And His children will have a place of refuge.

PROVERBS 14:26

The name of the LORD is a strong tower;
The righteous run to it and are safe.

PROVERBS 18:10

When you pass through the waters, I will be
    with you;
And through the rivers, they shall not
    overflow you.
When you walk through the fire, you shall
    not be burned,
Nor shall the flame scorch you.   ISAIAH 43:2

Shelter

The eternal God is your refuge,
And underneath are the everlasting arms.

DEUTERONOMY 33:27a

I will both lie down in peace, and sleep;
For You alone, O LORD, make me dwell
in safety.

PSALM 4:8

You are my hiding place;
You shall preserve me from trouble;
You shall surround me with songs of
deliverance.

Selah

PSALM 32:7

The LORD also will roar from Zion,
And utter His voice from Jerusalem;
The heavens and earth will shake;
But the LORD will be a shelter for
His people,
And the strength of the children of Israel.

JOEL 3:16

But the Lord is faithful, who will establish
you and guard you from the evil one.

2 THESSALONIANS 3:3

Guidance in Business

And you shall remember the LORD your
God, for it is He who gives you power to get
wealth, that He may establish His covenant
which He swore to your fathers, as it is
this day.   DEUTERONOMY 8:18

You shall not pervert justice; you shall not
show partiality, nor take a bribe, for a bribe
blinds the eyes of the wise and twists the
words of the righteous. You shall follow what
is altogether just, that you may live and
inherit the land which the LORD your God is
giving you.   DEUTERONOMY 16:19, 20

Now it shall come to pass, if you diligently
obey the voice of the LORD your God, to
observe carefully all His commandments
which I command you today, that the LORD
your God will set you high above all nations
of the earth. And all these blessings shall
come upon you and overtake you, because
you obey the voice of the LORD your God
.   DEUTERONOMY 28:1, 2

Blessed is the man
Who walks not in the counsel of the
    ungodly,
    Nor stands in the path of sinners,
    Nor sits in the seat of the scornful;
But his delight is in the law of the LORD,
    And in His law he meditates day and
    night.
He shall be like a tree
    Planted by the rivers of water,
    That brings forth its fruit in its season,
    Whose leaf also shall not wither;
And whatever he does shall prosper.

PSALM 1:1–3

Masters, give your bondservants what is just
and fair, knowing that you also have a
Master in heaven.   COLOSSIANS 4:1

Wisdom

Happy is the man who finds wisdom,
And the man who gains understanding;
For her proceeds are better than the profits
    of silver,
And her gain than fine gold.
She is more precious than rubies,
And all the things you may desire cannot
    compare with her.   PROVERBS 3:13–15

The fear of the LORD is the beginning
    of wisdom,
And the knowledge of the Holy One
    is understanding.   PROVERBS 9:10

The mouth of the righteous brings
    forth wisdom,
But the perverse tongue will be cut out.
                      PROVERBS 10:31

He who heeds the word wisely will
    find good,
And whoever trusts in the LORD, happy
    is he.   PROVERBS 16:20

If any of you lacks wisdom, let him ask of
God, who gives to all liberally and without
reproach, and it will be given to him.
                            JAMES 1:5

Peace of Mind

The LORD bless you and keep you;
The LORD make His face shine upon you,
And be gracious to you;
The LORD lift up His countenance upon you,
And give you peace.   NUMBERS 6:24–26

You will keep him in perfect peace,
Whose mind is stayed on You,
Because he trusts in You.   ISAIAH 26:3

The work of righteousness will be peace,
And the effect of righteousness, quietness
   and assurance forever.   ISAIAH 32:17

Therefore, having been justified by faith, we
have peace with God through our Lord Jesus
Christ.   ROMANS 5:1

And the peace of God, which surpasses all
understanding, will guard your hearts and
minds through Christ Jesus.   PHILIPPIANS 4:7

Hope
When
You
Are . . .

Sick or Infirm

The LORD will strengthen him on his bed
    of illness;
You will sustain him on his sickbed.

PSALM 41:3

But He was wounded for our
    transgressions,
He was bruised for our iniquities;
The chastisement for our peace was
    upon Him,
And by His stripes we are healed.   ISAIAH 53:5

Therefore we do not lose heart. Even
though our outward man is perishing, yet
the inward man is being renewed day by
day. For our light affliction, which is but for a
moment, is working for us a far more
exceeding and eternal weight of glory, while
we do not look at the things which are seen,
but at the things which are not seen. For the
things which are seen are temporary, but
the things which are not seen are eternal.

2 CORINTHIANS 4:16–18

And He said to me, "My grace is sufficient
for you, for My strength is made perfect in
weakness." Therefore most gladly I will
rather boast in my infirmities, that the
power of Christ may rest upon me.

2 CORINTHIANS 12:9

Is anyone among you sick? Let him call for the elders of the church, and let them pray over him, anointing him with oil in the name of the Lord. And the prayer of faith will save the sick, and the Lord will raise him up. And if he has committed sins, he will be forgiven. Confess your trespasses to one another, and pray for one another, that you may be healed. The effective, fervent prayer of a righteous man avails much.   JAMES 5:14–16

Seriously or Terminally Ill

The LORD is my shepherd;
I shall not want.
He makes me to lie down in green pastures;
He leads me beside the still waters.
He restores my soul;
He leads me in the paths of righteousness
For His name's sake.

Yea, though I walk through the valley of the
    shadow of death,
I will fear no evil;
For You are with me;
Your rod and Your staff, they comfort me.

PSALM 23:1–4

God is our refuge and strength,
A very present help in trouble.   PSALM 46:1

Hear my cry, O God;
Attend to my prayer.
From the end of the earth I will
cry to You,
When my heart is overwhelmed;
Lead me to the rock that is higher than I.

For You have been a shelter for me,
A strong tower from the enemy.
I will abide in Your tabernacle forever;
I will trust in the shelter of
Your wings.   Selah

PSALM 61:1–4

The LORD is near to all who call
upon Him,
To all who call upon Him in truth.

PSALM 145:18

Surely He has borne our griefs
And carried our sorrows;
Yet we esteemed Him stricken,
Smitten by God, and afflicted.
But He was wounded for our
transgressions,
He was bruised for our iniquities;
The chastisement for our peace was
upon Him,
And by His stripes we are healed.

ISAIAH 53:4, 5

Suffering

Cast your burden on the LORD,
And He shall sustain you;
He shall never permit the righteous
    to be moved.   PSALM 55:22

He gives power to the weak,
And to those who have no might He
    increases strength.
Even the youths shall faint and
    be weary,
And the young men shall utterly fall,
But those who wait on the LORD
Shall renew their strength;
They shall mount up with wings
    like eagles,
They shall run and not be weary,
They shall walk and not faint.   ISAIAH 40:29–31

We are children of God, and if children,
then heirs—heirs of God and joint heirs
with Christ, if indeed we suffer with Him,
that we may also be glorified together. For I
consider that the sufferings of this present
time are not worthy to be compared with
the glory which shall be revealed in us.

ROMANS 8:16b–18

Blessed be the God and Father of our Lord Jesus Christ, the Father of mercies and God of all comfort, who comforts us in all our tribulation, that we may be able to comfort those who are in any trouble, with the comfort with which we ourselves are comforted by God. For as the sufferings of Christ abound in us, so our consolation also abounds through Christ.   2 CORINTHIANS 1:3–5

Yet indeed I also count all things loss for the excellence of the knowledge of Christ Jesus my Lord . . . that I may know Him and the power of His resurrection, and the fellowship of His sufferings, being conformed to His death, if, by any means, I may attain to the resurrection from the dead.

PHILIPPIANS 3:8a, 10, 11

Being Persecuted

Who shall separate us from the love of Christ? Shall tribulation, or distress, or persecution, or famine, or nakedness, or peril, or sword? As it is written:

"For Your sake we are killed all day long;
We are accounted as sheep for the
    slaughter."

Yet in all these things we are more than conquerors through Him who loved us.

ROMANS 8:35–37

For we do not want you to be ignorant, brethren, of our trouble which came to us in Asia: that we were burdened beyond measure, above strength, so that we despaired even of life. Yes, we had the sentence of death in ourselves, that we should not trust in ourselves but in God who raises the dead, who delivered us from so great a death, and does deliver us; in whom we trust that He will still deliver us, you also helping together in prayer for us, that thanks may be given by many persons on our behalf for the gift granted to us through many.   2 CORINTHIANS 1:8–11

But the Lord is faithful, who will establish you and guard you from the evil one.

2 THESSALONIANS 3:3

Beloved, do not think it strange concerning the fiery trial which is to try you, as though some strange thing happened to you; but rejoice to the extent that you partake of Christ's sufferings, that when His glory is revealed, you may also be glad with exceeding joy. If you are reproached for the name of Christ, blessed are you, for the Spirit of glory and of God rests upon you. On their part He is blasphemed, but on your part He is glorified.   1 PETER 4:12–14

And they overcame him by the blood of the Lamb and by the word of their testimony, and they did not love their lives to the death.   REVELATION 12:11

Aging

I have been young, and now am old;
Yet I have not seen the righteous forsaken,
Nor his descendants begging bread.
                                        PSALM 37:25

O God, You have taught me from
     my youth;
And to this day I declare Your
     wondrous works.
Now also when I am old and grayheaded,
O God, do not forsake me,
Until I declare Your strength to
     this generation,
Your power to everyone who is to come.
                                    PSALM 71:17, 18

With long life I will satisfy him,
And show him My salvation.   PSALM 91:16

Those who are planted in the house
     of the LORD
Shall flourish in the courts of our God.
They shall still bear fruit in old age;
They shall be fresh and flourishing.
                                    PSALM 92:13, 14

Even to your old age, I am He,
And even to gray hairs I will
carry you!
I have made, and I will bear;
Even I will carry, and will
deliver you.   ISAIAH 46:4

Under Financial Stress

The LORD is my shepherd;
I shall not want.   PSALM 23:1

Oh, fear the LORD, you His saints!
There is no want to those who
fear Him.
The young lions lack and suffer
hunger;
But those who seek the LORD
shall not lack any good thing.
                           PSALM 34:9, 10

Honor the LORD with your
possessions,
And with the firstfruits of all your
increase;
So your barns will be filled
with plenty,
And your vats will overflow with
new wine.   PROVERBS 3:9, 10

He who is faithful in what is least is faithful also in much; and he who is unjust in what is least is unjust also in much.   LUKE 16:10

But this I say: He who sows sparingly will also reap sparingly, and he who sows bountifully will also reap bountifully. So let each one give as he purposes in his heart, not grudgingly or of necessity; for God loves a cheerful giver. And God is able to make all grace abound toward you, that you, always having all sufficiency in all things, may have an abundance for every good work.
2 CORINTHIANS 9:6–8

Experiencing Injustice

He administers justice for the fatherless and the widow, and loves the stranger, giving him food and clothing.   DEUTERONOMY 10:18

So the poor have hope,
And injustice shuts her mouth.   JOB 5:16

The humble He guides in justice,
And the humble He teaches His way.
PSALM 25:9

Many seek the ruler's favor,
But justice for man comes from the LORD.
PROVERBS 29:26

The LORD is righteous in her midst,
He will do no unrighteousness.
Every morning He brings His justice to light;
He never fails,
But the unjust knows no shame.

ZEPHANIAH 3:5

Facing Difficulties

Be strong and of good courage, do not fear
nor be afraid of them; for the LORD your
God, He is the One who goes with you. He
will not leave you nor forsake you.

DEUTERONOMY 31:6

Thus says the LORD who made you
And formed you from the womb, who will
    help you:
"Fear not, O Jacob My servant;
And you, Jeshurun, whom I have chosen.
For I will pour water on him who is thirsty,
And floods on the dry ground;
I will pour My Spirit on your descendants,
And My blessing on your offspring."

ISAIAH 44:2, 3

We are hard-pressed on every side, yet not crushed; we are perplexed, but not in despair; persecuted, but not forsaken; struck down, but not destroyed.

2 CORINTHIANS 4:8, 9

I can do all things through Christ who strengthens me.

PHILIPPIANS 4:13

Therefore humble yourselves under the mighty hand of God, that He may exalt you in due time, casting all your care upon Him, for He cares for you.

1 PETER 5:6, 7

Hope
to
Overcome

Being Abandoned

Be strong and of good courage, do not fear
nor be afraid of them; for the LORD your
God, He is the One who goes with you. He
will not leave you nor forsake you.

DEUTERONOMY 31:6

Do not be afraid, nor be dismayed, for the
LORD your God is with you wherever you go.

JOSHUA 1:9b

For the LORD will not forsake His people, for
His great name's sake, because it has
pleased the LORD to make you His people.

I SAMUEL 12:22

A father of the fatherless, a defender
    of widows,
Is God in His holy habitation.   PSALM 68:5

Can a woman forget her nursing child,
And not have compassion on the son of
    her womb?
Surely they may forget,
Yet I will not forget you.
See, I have inscribed you on the palms of
    My hands;
Your walls are continually before Me.

ISAIAH 49:15, 16

A Negative Environment

Blessed is the man
Who walks not in the counsel of
    the ungodly,
  Nor stands in the path of sinners,
  Nor sits in the seat of the scornful;
But his delight is in the law of the LORD,
  And in His law he meditates day
    and night.   PSALM 1:1, 2

But the salvation of the righteous is from
    the LORD;
He is their strength in the time of trouble.
And the LORD shall help them and
    deliver them;
He shall deliver them from the wicked,
And save them,
Because they trust in Him.   PSALM 37:39, 40

"No weapon formed against you shall
    prosper,
And every tongue which rises against you
    in judgment
You shall condemn.
This is the heritage of the servants
    of the LORD,
And their righteousness is from Me,"
Says the LORD.   ISAIAH 54:17

Love suffers long and is kind; love does not
envy; love does not parade itself, is not
puffed up; does not behave rudely, does
not seek its own, is not provoked, thinks no
evil; does not rejoice in iniquity, but rejoices in the truth; bears all things, believes all
things, hopes all things, endures all things.
Love never fails.   1 CORINTHIANS 13:4–8a

Finally, brethren, whatever things are true,
whatever things are noble, whatever things
are just, whatever things are pure, whatever
things are lovely, whatever things are of
good report, if there is any virtue and if
there is anything praiseworthy—meditate
on these things.   PHILIPPIANS 4:8

Words You Don't Mean

Keep your tongue from evil,
And your lips from speaking deceit.
                              PSALM 34:13

In the multitude of words sin is not lacking,
But he who restrains his lips is wise.
The tongue of the righteous is choice silver;
The heart of the wicked is worth little.
The lips of the righteous feed many,
But fools die for lack of wisdom.
                              PROVERBS 10:19–21

Whoever guards his mouth
    and tongue
Keeps his soul from troubles.   PROVERBS 21:23

Strength and honor are her
    clothing;
She shall rejoice in time to come.
She opens her mouth with
    wisdom,
And on her tongue is the
    law of kindness.   PROVERBS 31:25, 26

But no man can tame the tongue. It is an
unruly evil, full of deadly poison. With it we
bless our God and Father, and with it we
curse men, who have been made in the
similitude of God. Out of the same mouth
proceed blessing and cursing. My brethren,
these things ought not to be so.   JAMES 3:8–10

The Threats of the Enemy

And the God of peace will crush Satan
under your feet shortly. The grace of our
Lord Jesus Christ be with you. Amen.
                                ROMANS 16:20

Finally, my brethren, be strong in the Lord and in the power of His might. Put on the whole armor of God, that you may be able to stand against the wiles of the devil. For we do not wrestle against flesh and blood, but against principalities, against powers, against the rulers of the darkness of this age, against spiritual hosts of wickedness in the heavenly places.   EPHESIANS 6:10–12

But the Lord is faithful, who will establish you and guard you from the evil one.

2 THESSALONIANS 3:3

Therefore submit to God. Resist the devil and he will flee from you.   JAMES 4:7

You are of God, little children, and have overcome them, because He who is in you is greater than he who is in the world.

1 JOHN 4:4

Addiction

The horse is prepared for the day of battle, But deliverance is of the LORD.

PROVERBS 21:31

Therefore if the Son makes you free, you shall be free indeed.   JOHN 8:36

Yet in all these things we are more than conquerors through Him who loved us.

ROMANS 8:37

Stand fast therefore in the liberty by which Christ has made us free, and do not be entangled again with a yoke of bondage.

GALATIANS 5:1

For we do not have a High Priest who cannot sympathize with our weaknesses, but was in all points tempted as we are, yet without sin. Let us therefore come boldly to the throne of grace, that we may obtain mercy and find grace to help in time of need.

HEBREWS 4:15, 16

Lust

Let us walk properly, as in the day, not in revelry and drunkenness, not in lewdness and lust, not in strife and envy. ROMANS 13:13

I say then: Walk in the Spirit, and you shall not fulfill the lust of the flesh. GALATIANS 5:16

For this is the will of God, your sanctification: that you should abstain from sexual immorality; that each of you should know how to possess his own vessel in sanctification and honor. 1 THESSALONIANS 4:3, 4

For the grace of God that brings salvation has appeared to all men, teaching us that, denying ungodliness and worldly lusts, we should live soberly, righteously, and godly in the present age, looking for the blessed hope and glorious appearing of our great God and Savior Jesus Christ, who gave Himself for us, that He might redeem us from every lawless deed and purify for Himself His own special people, zealous for good works.

TITUS 2:11–14

Do not love the world or the things in the world. If anyone loves the world, the love of the Father is not in him. For all that is in the world—the lust of the flesh, the lust of the eyes, and the pride of life—is not of the Father but is of the world. And the world is passing away, and the lust of it; but he who does the will of God abides forever.

1 JOHN 2:15–17

A Critical Spirit

Search me, O God, and know my heart;
Try me, and know my anxieties;
And see if there is any wicked way in me,
And lead me in the way everlasting.

PSALM 139:23, 24

Set a guard, O LORD, over my
    mouth;
Keep watch over the door
    of my lips.   PSALM 141:3

Judge not, that you be not judged.
                      MATTHEW 7:1

And be kind to one another, tenderhearted,
forgiving one another, even as God in Christ
forgave you.   EPHESIANS 4:32

Let your speech always be with grace, sea-
soned with salt, that you may know how you
ought to answer each one.   COLOSSIANS 4:6

Abortion

For I am the LORD who heals you.
                      EXODUS 15:26b

But You, O LORD, are a shield for me,
My glory and the One who lifts
    up my head.
I cried to the LORD with my voice,
And He heard me from His holy hill.   Selah

I lay down and slept;
I awoke, for the LORD sustained me.
                      PSALM 3:3–5

He heals the brokenhearted
And binds up their wounds.   PSALM 147:3

I, even I, am He who blots out your
transgressions for My own sake;
And I will not remember your sins.

ISAIAH 43:25

In Him we have redemption through His
blood, the forgiveness of sins, according to
the riches of His grace which He made to
abound toward us in all wisdom and
prudence. EPHESIANS 1:7, 8

Mental Illness

The LORD also will be a refuge for
the oppressed,
A refuge in times of trouble.
And those who know Your name will put
their trust in You;
For You, LORD, have not forsaken those who
seek You. PSALM 9:9, 10

He sent His word and healed them,
And delivered them from their destructions.

PSALM 107:20

When you lie down, you will not
   be afraid;
Yes, you will lie down and your sleep will
   be sweet.
Do not be afraid of sudden terror,
Nor of trouble from the wicked when
   it comes;
For the LORD will be your confidence,
And will keep your foot from being caught.

PROVERBS 3:24–26

Be anxious for nothing, but in everything by
prayer and supplication, with thanksgiving,
let your requests be made known to God;
and the peace of God, which surpasses all
understanding, will guard your hearts and
minds through Christ Jesus.   PHILIPPIANS 4:6, 7

For God has not given us a spirit of fear, but
of power and of love and of a sound mind.

2 TIMOTHY 1:7

A Mistake

Brethren, if a man is overtaken in any tres-
pass, you who are spiritual restore such a
one in a spirit of gentleness, considering
yourself lest you also be tempted. Bear one
another's burdens, and so fulfill the law of
Christ.   GALATIANS 6:1, 2

Brethren, I do not count myself to have apprehended; but one thing I do, forgetting those things which are behind and reaching forward to those things which are ahead, I press toward the goal for the prize of the upward call of God in Christ Jesus.

PHILIPPIANS 3:13, 14

Humble yourselves in the sight of the Lord, and He will lift you up.   JAMES 4:10

Therefore humble yourselves under the mighty hand of God, that He may exalt you in due time, casting all your care upon Him, for He cares for you.   1 PETER 5:6, 7

If we confess our sins, He is faithful and just to forgive us our sins and to cleanse us from all unrighteousness.   1 JOHN 1:9

Temptation

No temptation has overtaken you except such as is common to man; but God is faithful, who will not allow you to be tempted beyond what you are able, but with the temptation will also make the way of escape, that you may be able to bear it.

1 CORINTHIANS 10:13

I say then: Walk in the Spirit, and you shall not fulfill the lust of the flesh.   GALATIANS 5:16

For in that He Himself has suffered, being tempted, He is able to aid those who are tempted.   HEBREWS 2:18

Blessed is the man who endures temptation; for when he has been approved, he will receive the crown of life which the Lord has promised to those who love Him.

JAMES 1:12

Now to Him who is able to keep you
    from stumbling,
And to present you faultless
Before the presence of His glory with
    exceeding joy,
To God our Savior,
Who alone is wise,
Be glory and majesty,
Dominion and power,
Both now and forever.
Amen.   JUDE 24, 25

Rebellion

For rebellion is as the sin of witchcraft,
And stubbornness is as iniquity
        and idolatry.   1 SAMUEL 15:23a

To the Lord our God belong mercy and forgiveness, though we have rebelled against Him.
                                    DANIEL 9:9

Therefore do not let sin reign in your mortal body, that you should obey it in its lusts. And do not present your members as instruments of unrighteousness to sin, but present yourselves to God as being alive from the dead, and your members as instruments of righteousness to God.

ROMANS 6:12, 13

Obey those who rule over you, and be submissive, for they watch out for your souls, as those who must give account. Let them do so with joy and not with grief, for that would be unprofitable for you.   HEBREWS 13:17

Therefore gird up the loins of your mind, be sober, and rest your hope fully upon the grace that is to be brought to you at the revelation of Jesus Christ; as obedient children, not conforming yourselves to the former lusts, as in your ignorance; but as He who called you is holy, you also be holy in all your conduct, because it is written, "Be holy, for I am holy."   1 PETER 1:13–16

Sin

Have mercy upon me, O God,
According to Your lovingkindness;
According to the multitude of Your tender
    mercies,
Blot out my transgressions.
Wash me thoroughly from my iniquity,
And cleanse me from my sin.

For I acknowledge my transgressions,
And my sin is always before me.

PSALM 51:1–3

Let the wicked forsake his way,
And the unrighteous man his thoughts;
Let him return to the LORD,
And He will have mercy on him;
And to our God,
For He will abundantly pardon.   ISAIAH 55:7

Behold, the LORD's hand is not shortened,
That it cannot save;
Nor His ear heavy,
That it cannot hear.   ISAIAH 59:1

Therefore we also, since we are surrounded by so great a cloud of witnesses, let us lay aside every weight, and the sin which so easily ensnares us, and let us run with endurance the race that is set before us, looking unto Jesus, the author and finisher of our faith.   HEBREWS 12:1, 2

If we confess our sins, He is faithful and just to forgive us our sins and to cleanse us from all unrighteousness.   1 JOHN 1:9

Celebrating Your Hope

Through Praise

Stand up and bless the LORD your God
Forever and ever!

Blessed be Your glorious name,
Which is exalted above all blessing
    and praise!
You alone are the LORD;
You have made heaven,
The heaven of heavens, with all
    their host,
The earth and everything on it,
The seas and all that is in them,
And You preserve them all.
The host of heaven worships You.

NEHEMIAH 9:5b, 6

You have turned for me my mourning
    into dancing;
You have put off my sackcloth and clothed
    me with gladness,
To the end that my glory may sing praise to
    You and not be silent.
O LORD my God, I will give thanks to
    You forever.

PSALM 30:11, 12

Every day I will bless You,
And I will praise Your name forever
    and ever.
Great is the LORD, and greatly to be praised;
And His greatness is unsearchable.

One generation shall praise Your works
    to another,
And shall declare Your mighty acts.

PSALM 145:2–4

Praise the LORD!
For it is good to sing praises to our God;
For it is pleasant, and praise is beautiful.

PSALM 147:1

Then I looked, and I heard the voice of
many angels around the throne, the living
creatures, and the elders . . . saying with a
loud voice:

"Worthy is the Lamb who was slain
To receive power and riches and wisdom,
And strength and honor and glory
    and blessing!"

And every creature which is in heaven and
on the earth and under the earth and such
as are in the sea, and all that are in them, I
heard saying:

"Blessing and honor and glory and power
Be to Him who sits on the throne,
And to the Lamb, forever and ever!"

REVELATION 5:11a–13

Through Worship

Give unto the LORD, O you mighty ones,
Give unto the LORD glory and strength.
Give unto the LORD the glory due to
     His name;
Worship the LORD in the beauty
     of holiness.   PSALM 29:1, 2

Your mercy, O LORD, is in the
     heavens;
Your faithfulness reaches to
     the clouds.
Your righteousness is like the great
     mountains;
Your judgments are a great deep;
O LORD, You preserve man
     and beast.

How precious is Your lovingkindness,
     O God!
Therefore the children of men put
     their trust under the shadow of
     Your wings.
They are abundantly satisfied with the
     fullness of Your house,
And You give them drink from the river of
     Your pleasures.   PSALM 36:5–8

Say to God,
"How awesome are Your works!
Through the greatness of
Your power
Your enemies shall submit themselves
to You.
All the earth shall worship You
And sing praises to You;
They shall sing praises to
Your name." Selah

Come and see the works of God;
He is awesome in His doing toward
the sons of men. PSALM 66:3–5

For You are great, and do wondrous
things;
You alone are God.

Teach me Your way, O LORD;
I will walk in Your truth;
Unite my heart to fear Your name.
I will praise You, O Lord my God, with all
my heart,
And I will glorify Your name forevermore.

PSALM 86:10–12

They sing the song of Moses, the servant of
God, and the song of the Lamb, saying:

"Great and marvelous are Your works,
Lord God Almighty!
Just and true are Your ways,
O King of the saints!
Who shall not fear You, O Lord, and glorify
Your name?
For You alone are holy.
For all nations shall come and worship
before You,
For Your judgments have been manifested."

REVELATION 15:3, 4

Through Thanksgiving

Oh, give thanks to the LORD!
Call upon His name;
Make known His deeds among the peoples!
Sing to Him, sing psalms to Him;
Talk of all His wondrous works!
Glory in His holy name;
Let the hearts of those rejoice who seek
the LORD!
Seek the LORD and His strength;
Seek His face evermore! 1 CHRONICLES 16:8–11

Yours, O LORD, is the greatness,
The power and the glory,
The victory and the majesty;
For all that is in heaven and in earth
     is Yours;
Yours is the kingdom, O LORD,
And You are exalted as head over all.
Both riches and honor come from You,
And You reign over all.
In Your hand is power and might;
In Your hand it is to make great
And to give strength to all.

Now therefore, our God,
We thank You
And praise Your glorious name.

I CHRONICLES 29:11–13

I will praise the name of God with a song,
And will magnify Him with thanksgiving.

PSALM 69:30

Enter into His gates with thanksgiving,
And into His courts with praise.
Be thankful to Him, and bless His name.
For the LORD is good;
His mercy is everlasting,
And His truth endures to all generations.

PSALM 100:4, 5

All the angels . . . worshiped God, saying:

"Amen! Blessing and glory and wisdom,
Thanksgiving and honor and power
    and might,
Be to our God forever and ever.
Amen."   REVELATION 7:11, 12

Through Exaltation

The LORD is my strength and song,
And He has become my salvation;
He is my God, and I will praise Him;
My father's God, and I will exalt Him.
                            EXODUS 15:2

I will bless the LORD at all times;
His praise shall continually be in my mouth.
My soul shall make its boast in the LORD;
The humble shall hear of it and be glad.
Oh, magnify the LORD with me,
And let us exalt His name together.
                            PSALM 34:1–3

Exalt the LORD our God,
And worship at His footstool—
He is holy.   PSALM 99:5

You are my God, and I will praise You;
You are my God, I will exalt You.

Oh, give thanks to the LORD, for He is good!
For His mercy endures forever.

PSALM 118:28, 29

O LORD, You are my God.
I will exalt You,
I will praise Your name,
For You have done wonderful things;
Your counsels of old are faithfulness
    and truth.

ISAIAH 25:1

Through Rejoicing

But let all those rejoice who put their trust
    in You;
Let them ever shout for joy, because You
    defend them;
Let those also who love Your name
Be joyful in You.

PSALM 5:11

You will show me the path of life;
In Your presence is fullness of joy;
At Your right hand are pleasures
    forevermore.

PSALM 16:11

Make a joyful shout to the LORD, all
  you lands!
Serve the LORD with gladness;
Come before His presence with singing.
Know that the LORD, He is God;
It is He who has made us, and not
  we ourselves;
We are His people and the sheep of
  His pasture.

Enter into His gates with thanksgiving,
And into His courts with praise.
Be thankful to Him, and bless His name.

PSALM 100:1–4

So the ransomed of the LORD shall return,
And come to Zion with singing,
With everlasting joy on their heads.
They shall obtain joy and gladness;
Sorrow and sighing shall flee away.

ISAIAH 51:11

Rejoice always, pray without ceasing, in
everything give thanks; for this is the will of
God in Christ Jesus for you.

1 THESSALONIANS 5:16–18

Through Your Thoughts

Let the words of my mouth and the
    meditation of my heart
Be acceptable in Your sight,
O LORD, my strength and my Redeemer.

PSALM 19:14

I will sing to the LORD as long as I live;
I will sing praise to my God while I have
    my being.
May my meditation be sweet to Him;
I will be glad in the LORD.   PSALM 104:33, 34

Oh, how I love Your law!
It is my meditation all the day.   PSALM 119:97

LORD, my heart is not haughty,
Nor my eyes lofty.
Neither do I concern myself with
    great matters,
Nor with things too profound for me.

Surely I have calmed and quieted my soul,
Like a weaned child with his mother;
Like a weaned child is my soul within me.

O Israel, hope in the LORD
From this time forth and forever.

PSALM 131:1–3

Therefore gird up the loins of your mind, be sober, and rest your hope fully upon the grace that is to be brought to you at the revelation of Jesus Christ.   1 PETER 1:13

Through Singing

Then Miriam the prophetess, the sister of Aaron, took the timbrel in her hand; and all the women went out after her with timbrels and with dances. And Miriam answered them:

"Sing to the LORD,
For He has triumphed gloriously!
The horse and its rider
He has thrown into the sea!"   EXODUS 15:20, 21

Sing to the LORD, all the earth;
Proclaim the good news of His salvation
    from day to day.
Declare His glory among the nations,
His wonders among all peoples.

For the LORD is great and greatly to
    be praised;
He is also to be feared above all gods.
                              1 CHRONICLES 16:23–25

Sing to Him, sing psalms to Him;
Talk of all His wondrous works!
Glory in His holy name;
Let the hearts of those rejoice who seek
    the LORD!
Seek the LORD and His strength;
Seek His face evermore!   PSALM 105:2–4

Praise the LORD!

Sing to the LORD a new song,
And His praise in the assembly of saints.

Let Israel rejoice in their Maker;
Let the children of Zion be joyful in
    their King.
Let them praise His name with the dance;
Let them sing praises to Him with the
    timbrel and harp.
For the LORD takes pleasure in His people;
He will beautify the humble with salvation.

Let the saints be joyful in glory;
Let them sing aloud on their beds.

PSALM 149:1–5

Sing, O daughter of Zion!
Shout, O Israel!
Be glad and rejoice with all
    your heart,
O daughter of Jerusalem! . . .

The LORD your God in your midst,
The Mighty One, will save;
He will rejoice over you with
    gladness,
He will quiet you with His love,
He will rejoice over you
    with singing.   ZEPHANIAH 3:14, 17